# In The Heart Of Blooming Flower

S. Saumya

BookLeaf Publishing

India | USA | UK

Made with ❤ on the BookLeaf Publishing Platform
www.bookleafpub.in
www.bookleafpub.com

# Dedication

For those who will rise again and water themselves continuously, trusting that they will eventually bloom.

# Preface

This book is a collection of poems I wrote during my adolescence, when days had slipped by like seasons.

Many of these poems are inspired by the world around me, a passing conversation, a stranger's smile, or a friend's sorrow; and others are drawn from my own experiences. These poems are about life in all its layers, friendship, happiness, loss, love, hope, and everything in between.

I never thought of writing a book. I simply wrote what I saw, heard, or felt, trying not to let those moments evaporate. However, as my teenage years are about to be over, I discovered that I am someone who wishes to save it all, not only the good, but the whole spectrum: the tears, the sadness, or the smiles of those I love and the ones who love me. Writing is a way I have kept the emotions alive, the same way you keep flowers between the pages of a diary or a book, just as a memory to revisit them.

And so, this book becomes a home for it all.


S. Saumya

# Acknowledgements

This book would not have been possible without a sky full of people who helped me believe in the beauty of my words.

My deepest gratitude to BookLeaf Publishing for being the platform that made my dream possible, a dream I can now hold in my hands. Thank you for providing a home for my words.

A big thank you to my dearest parents for being the backbone of my dreams and aspirations, and for their constant love, affection and care.

To my sibling, thank you for being the quiet support I never had to ask for, and for designing the cover of this book, your creativity brought this book to life.

And a heartfelt thank you to my cousin for reviewing my poems and helping me to shape this collection into its final form.

To my friends and readers who have found pieces of themselves in the words I write, your love and encouragement lit the path for me, even on the days I doubted myself.

Finally, I want to express my gratitude to you, the reader, for holding these pages. If you see fragments of yourself in these pages, even for once, then I would like to believe I have done more than I ever dreamed of.

# If Someone Has Not Told You Yet

Oceans in your eyes,
stars in your dreams,
flowers in your heart,
I don't know what you are,
if not a work of art.

Abundant colours of your emotions,
and truly,
an enthralling creation of God,
sent on the earth
from the brink of heaven.

# My Enigmatic Rainbow

2

Violet for my journal,
Indigo for my pen,
Blue for my oceans,
Yellow for my sunrise,
Orange for my sunset,
Red for my fire,
And white for my soul,
So, tell me, dear heart,
What's all this black for?

# In Praise of You

Give your beauty a chance, as you must.
Embrace your inner spark,
and the colour of your eyes and skin,
as if there's a world waiting outside for you,
your kindness, and your little shy grins.

You, are your muse, a poetic devotion,
and a masterpiece in motion.
In a world that may not see your worth,
I, as a poet, declare you a diamond,
a gem of brilliance, and a treasure from birth.

# The Daydreamer

As she sits in her silence,
while people pass through the lanes,
she daydreams of the world of Rapunzel and her lover.

As she sits surrounded by the greenery,
gazing at the sky,
she chooses no one but herself.

As she watches the time tick by,
she wishes to leave this reality,
and dance in another paradise.

# The Quiet Hope of Love

I preach friends-to-lovers
the way the father preaches the Bible,
with unwavering faith,
as if it were a gospel of my own.
I see my friend and hold the quiet hope of,
"Oh, we would look so good together."
I feel butterflies take flight
within my very existence,
as each one giggles when he looks at me in a way,
he isn't supposed to.

When my mother often asks me
the look I always talk about.
and I tell her:
"Dear mom, It's the look
where my eyes carry the stars,
and he longs to count each one of them
as if untangling a secret sky.
It's the look that says
I am the sunshine he waits for every night,
the look that whispers,
If only we could be together.
If only I could be his, and he could be mine."

# My Coffee, and I

He said, "I like you."
I paused, watching my hot coffee grow cold.
Those three words hung in the air.
It was once a distant dream,
For a girl who sat in a coffeehouse,
Hoping and wishing,
"I wish he could see me as more than just a friend."

I craved love, the romantic kind,
Having had my coffee mugs filled with the Platonic ones.
I did not desire the moon, the stars, or flowers,
Only him, beside me,
In my joy and my melancholic hours.
But now, hearing those words,
I found myself speechless,
With nothing left to say.

My warm coffee had already turned cold,
And the coffeehouse,
With its lack of vintage charm,
Suddenly felt out of place.
I left it all there,
The unspoken words, my affection,
And my love for my favourite coffee.

Now, as I pass by that coffeehouse from time to time,
I see the reflection of my past self
While my eyes turn blue.
I ponder if my coffee might have stayed warm,
Had I whispered to him,
*"I like you too."*

# Half a Heart, Half a Lover

Can you ever separate the ashes from the graveyard?
Then how am I supposed to separate you from my memories?
Can you ever shoo away the birds singing at your doorstep?
Then how am I supposed to ignore you
Every time you appear before my life?
Can you ever hate the warmth of sunrays on winter days?
Then tell me, explain it to me,
Without words, only with your gaze,
How am I supposed to hate you?
Can you ever chase the moon, hold it still in the sky,
Beg it to remain whole, full and bright?
Then how can I ever ask you not to change?
Not to rip open my sadness,
And never to leave?
How could I ever ask you these questions?
I never had the right.
After all, I was merely a passing stranger,
Almost a friend,
And worst of all,
Barely... a *lover.*

# If Love Could

If love could fade the words I wrote,
I'd burn the poet's pen.
If love could take me away from you,
I'd never let it in.

If love could make me hate you,
I'd not do it again.
If love could taint the sweetest days,
I'd bear the aching wind.

If love could drown the dreams we dreamt,
I'd let them sink within.
If love could break my heart to dust,
I'd silence every hymn.

But if love couldn't be you,
Then truly,
I'd have never let it begin.

# Love is Blind

If I were to speak of love,
his name would grace my tongue.

If I were to whisper of betrayal,
his name would still be sung.

In every story, and every thought I frame,
I wonder if there's anything untouched by his name.

Though we are written with destinies apart,
everyone who knows me feels his absence in my heart.

As the old memories are replayed in my mind,
I lie down, lost, and wonder,
What is love, if it hasn't made you blind?

# Winters, That Still Wait for Her

Winters, when he wraps himself
in the tender memories of her love.
Winters, when her name softly settles on his lips,
like the warmth of hot chocolate
swirling in his coffee mug.

Winters, when he drapes himself in the same old hoodie,
clinging to the quiet hope,
that this December too,
she might just come, hold his hands,
and kiss away all his blues.

# Right Person, Wrong Timing

I fell in love with you when it was Summer,
and you fell in love with me when it was Spring.
Between Summer and Spring,
winter forgot to keep us warm,
that wove a bitter sting,
and hence, changed everything for you and me.
I didn't wait for you last December,
and perhaps that's why the nights of this December
keep me awake,
lost in the regrets of choices
that I could no longer remake.
We were the failures of love, prisoners of time
dreamers of the present, and companions of lies.
I lied when I said I hated you,
and you lied when you told me I wasn't your muse.
But I never hated you,
I hated the universe,
its cruel tricks, and its silent curse.
It made me a writer of love and despair,
weaving the stories of longing
that never truly led us anywhere.

# If There Exists a Next Life

If, by chance, there is a next life,
we get to have a restart,
what are the things you will do differently,
so that you will get to protect my heart,
and I will get to seek a home in your soul?

If, by chance, we meet in the next life,
I hope you are kind to me in the beginning,
as well as kind to yourself in the process,
so that there is no need to have the hope of next life,
and its different beginning to an end.

# A Hope So Excruciating

I am in search of someone
to strip me from the everlasting silhouette
of infinite chaos
wrapped around my soul.

For once, lays eyes on my scars
and perceives the house I had lived in
and finally builds me a home of tranquil love
that will be forever ours.

# Echoes of Solitude

At this stage of my life, I chuckle alone,
Where I return once in a while, a place of my own.
Surrounded by everyone, yet near to no one,
The ones I hold close slowly disappear.
Old friends rest in the graveyard of my memories,
Predictably, I see it unfold every time,
the heart's treacheries.
Hopes shattered, words in disarray,
In my bedsheets' creases, tears find their way.
Scattered pages tell the verses of beautiful lies,
"Why didn't you pick up my call?"
I deflect with sleepy eyes.
"Everything fine?" I nod and pretend.
"Why do you look so grief-stricken?"
I attribute it to a jaded trend.
In this labyrinth of emotions,
Disappointment takes hold,
Angry at myself or them,
The story that will never be told.
Persisting feelings, a weight I bear,
Past and present, blending together
In a tangle of despair.

# Voices in My Head

"You live in the past,"
Maybe the past is where I have lost myself.
"Don't live in the future,"
But that is where my ashes will lay.
"Try living in the present,"
Oh! Trust me, I do,
with the sparkle of hope burning bright.
With every passing year,
each of my birthday candles' flickering lights.

# I Don't Think So

Is it my fault that I was born
In a home with a little extra
Plates and spoons more than yours?
"I don't think so".

Is it my fault that my parents earn,
Earn enough so I can chase my dreams,
To see the world, to walk its edge,
And find my happiness?
"I don't think so".

Yes, I acknowledge I am born
With the privilege of basic necessities
You may still struggle for.
But what's the matter
If the privilege comes
From years of sweat,
Of hard-earned money,
Of dreams my parents sacrificed,
So that I can have one?

You will grow someday too,
Become a father
Or a mother.

You will earn for your children
And will give them every joy you can.

So why is it wrong
When my parents do the same for me?

Why, then, do you mock me?
Why, then, do you
Make my every comfort feel like a crime,
Turn my happiness into guilt,
Twist my laughter into shame,
As if I must apologize
For a life I didn't choose,
But simply inherited,
For a life woven
From my parents' dreams,
Threaded with the grace of God.
And, for a life I shouldn't carry all this guilt for.

# If I Could

If I could be a little less of who I am,
maybe then,
my ink wouldn't have turned red.
If I could silence the feeling of my own throat
crashing into my lungs,
maybe then,
I wouldn't choke on the weight of my own guilt.
If I could just let myself drown,
then maybe, just maybe,
I would breathe without feeling hollow,
eat without forcing it down,
run without dragging my own shadow,
talk without swallowing my own voice,
laugh without hearing the echo of my own emptiness.
And perhaps then,
I wouldn't have to watch myself fade
while the world keeps moving
as if I were never here,
maybe then,
I wouldn't have to watch my words blur away,
maybe then,
the story of my life would not take the whole sunset
to find its happy days.

# Serenity: A Home

Home is where silence speaks aloud,
echoing the depths of your heart.

Home is where your soul finds its person,
a refuge where tears intertwine with boundless love,
creating a symphony of emotions.

Home is heaven,
where happiness thrives amidst the sorrows,
painting your world with vibrant hues of bliss.

# The Warmth Between the Walls

My father does not speak a lot,
but I've seen it,
the quiet smile he wears
when I share
even my smallest wins.
And my mother,
who has spent most of her life
juggling through storms,
I've seen it,
the spark, the hope
that dances in her eyes.

Because they believe in me,
even as I falter in the frenzy of this world,
struggling to keep pace
with its breathless race,
they know,
I will find a voice to speak for myself,
I will find a path that follows my heart.
They gave me every joy,
and even handed me
pieces of their own smiles.

Ordinary, yet extraordinary,
with burdens of their own,
they still craft miracles each day,
turning the four walls of a house
into the warmth of a home.
A home,
stitched from their love.
A home,
I can always return to.
And a home,
that will forever be mine.

# God, & I

I seek shelter in God.
I ask God, "Why always me?"
as my tears accompany me
from my inner world to the outer one.
Yet, I still seek shelter in God.
For God is the goodness I believe in.
For who I was, I am, and will be,
there's no better version of me without Him.

# To Meet My Younger Self

Just like everyone else,
I want to meet my younger self at the coffee house too,
but I don't know which version of me I want to talk to.
Though they are me, they have grown with me within me.

I remember a version of them,
an extrovert, with the world in their hands.
And I know another,
perhaps more complex than the last,
quieter, more reserved,
with anxious linings wrapping around them,
choking their words, afraid to say them aloud.
I have lived both lives,
and now, two of me exist in the past.
So, I don't know which one to talk to.
I don't know which one to confide in.

Though both are blessed with the hearts of gold,
listeners like whispered prayers to God,
One is wrapped in sunshine, glowing each day,
while the other is hidden in the night,
with its own moonlight,
kept away from the warmth of sun rays.

Perhaps the three of us should meet,
not at the coffee house,
but here, in the quiet of my room,
where I write these fragmented words.
I want to see them both.

Though I have so much to tell each of them,
I would keep my prophecies locked in my heart,
and instead, I would hold them close,
and let my tears fall silently among us.
And if they ask me
what still drenches my heart in sorrow,
I will let them know it's not really the sorrow,
but neither would I call it the tears of joy.

I will tell them,
"It is simply who we are,
the weight of our past, the hopes of our future,
finding ways to breathe in the present.
Each one of us shaping our own moments and memories,
some with *love*, and some with *bravery*."